POWERFUL AFFIRMATIONS
for FemPreneurs

A SUCCESS TOOL FOR KINGDOM BUSINESS WOMEN

Visionary Nadia Francois

POWERFUL AFFIRMATIONS FOR FEMPRENEURS

A Success Tool for Kingdom Business Women

Visionary Author
Nadia Francois

Powerful Affirmations for FemPreneurs
Copyright © 2021 by

Heiress International Enterprises
www.heiressintl.com

All rights reserved. No part of this book may be reproduced or transmitted in any form or by any means without written permission from the author.

Printed in the USA

DEDICATION

This book is dedicated to every woman that is a business owner. Our position in this world is one that requires unshakeable faith and powerful prayer. The paths that are put before us are sometimes difficult to navigate. This book is a tool to help encourage and strengthen the female entrepreneur on her journey to building her FEMPIRE!!

INTRODUCTION

Powerful Affirmations for Fempreneurs is more than just a book, it's a faith-based declaration of victory for every woman building her business with boldness, purpose, and prayer.

This collection was written for you, the woman entrepreneur—the visionary, the trailblazer, the "kingdompreneur" who dares to dream big and believes that God has called her to create, lead, and prosper. The path of entrepreneurship is not always easy. It is filled with highs and lows, decisions that stretch us, and moments that demand unshakeable faith. That's why this book was created, to to serve as your pocket-sized spiritual boost when the road gets tough and your spirit needs a reminder of God's promises.

Inside these pages, you'll find affirmations and prayers penned by women who walk the same journey you do. These contributing authors have felt the late nights, carried the weight of vision, and clung to faith when resources were low but purpose was high. Each word is crafted to uplift, motivate, and realign your mindset with Kingdom purpose.

Whether you're launching a brand, running a thriving business, or rebuilding from the ground up, Powerful Affirmations for Fempreneurs will be your companion—your daily reminder that you are not alone, your business has a divine assignment, and your success is rooted in Christ.

Use this book to pray bold prayers. Speak these affirmations aloud. Declare victory over your life, your business, and your calling. Let it strengthen your spirit and fuel your focus.

Now is your time to build your FEMPIRE—with faith, prayer, and power. Let's walk this journey together, one promise at a time.

POWERFUL AFFRIMATIONS FOR FEMPRENEURS

AUTHOR DIRECTORY

DR. CATRINA PULLUM - FOREWORD

KIMBERLY ROWE - FOREWORD

NADIA FRANCOIS - VISIONARY

TONIA ASKINS

DANA AYO

BREONNA BAKER

DR. TONYA HILLIARD BATTIESTE

VASHITI BRATTON

ANGELICA CARMOUCHE

ELIZABETH CRAWFORD

MONICA JONES

MARILYN ODUENYI

CELESTE PAYNE

ERNEE PEPPERS

DR. ENOLA PILLARD

TAMURI RICHARDSON

SANDRA SANDERS

ADRIAN SMITH

DR. DIONNE SMITH

THINITRA SMITH

DR. SHANIKA STEWART

TOSHA WHITE

DR. FELESHIA BORSKEY-YOUNG

POWERFUL AFFIRMATIONS FOR FEMPRENEURS

TABLE OF CONTENTS

MY PURPOSE HAS POWER IN MY AFFIRMATIONS! ---------------- I
GRACE IN THE MIDST OF CHAOS -------------------------------------- VI
SUITING UP FOR BUSINESS
WITH THE ARMOR OF GOD -- 2
AFFIRMING AWARENESS,
ATTRACTION AND ABUNDANCE ----------------------------------- 10
DANA'S FEMFIRMATIONS -- 15
CROWNED WITH PURPOSE -- 19
I FRAME MY WORLD WITH MY WORDS! -------------------------- 23
LIVING VICTORIOUSLY --- 26
AFFIRMATIONS FOR A SPIRITUAL MENTALITY -------------------- 30
GOD'S QUEENDOM WOMAN --------------------------------------- 33
I AM WHO HE SAID, NOT WHAT THEY SAID ---------------------- 36
"SIS" --- 39
AFFIRMATIONS OF CREATIVITY ---------------------------------- 45
MRS. PEPPERS QUOTES --- 50
MY CUP RUNNETH OVER -- 54
BE RESPONSIBLE FOR WHO YOU TRULY ARE -------------------- 57
GOD'S PATH TO SUCCESS IN HIM -------------------------------- 61
SUNSHINE'S WORDS OF WISDOM --------------------------------- 64
I AM WHOLE -- 67
I MANIFEST! --- 71
SIS NOW IT'S YOUR TURN TO THRIVE ----------------------------- 74
I AM!! --- 78
PASSION AND PURPOSE FOR THE
PROMISES OF GOD--- 82

FOREWORD

My Purpose Has Power In My Affirmations!

Life can be changed forever with as little as a single expression or an inspiring word.

The dictionary defines an affirmation as an emotional support or encouragement. Why might this be important? Well, with so much hatred, bigotry, and negativity in the world, you do not have to look very hard to find someone very willing and able to tear you down. There are more people willing to tear you down than there are willing to lift you. Couple with the negative self-talk most of us do to ourselves, and you can see how needed and special a bit of positivity is to our mental health. As The Chain Breaker, Vision Strategist, and a Christian, I understand the Power of the words spoken into my life and the life of others.

FOREWORD CONT'D

The power of life and death are in the tongue. Words can bind us and words can set us free. I personally create at least one vision board every year, to set the tone for the year ahead. A key part of that vision casting is choosing words and phrases to remind me every time I see them what goals am I trying to accomplish; how am I supposed to see myself; what is the course and direction for my life. Over the years, I have found that my affirmations are necessary for my mental health like air and water are necessary for my physical health. Daily I declare and decree: I am a blessing! I expect blessings! I witness blessings! I express blessings! I manifest blessings! I experience blessings! This remarkable book written by an incredible group of women, will help you develop affirmations for yourself and your life. I want to share how I think you should use them.

 # FOREWORD CONT'D

You need to keep your words of encouragement around you to help keep you motivated and moving forward through life.

- Change up your lock screen or background on your phone to remind you of a key affirmation, or even cycle through a few of them.
- Write your affirmations on post-it notes or index cards and attach them to your bathroom or dresser mirror. That way not only are you saying your affirmations when you see them daily, you are also looking at yourself in the mirror and tying a vision of yourself saying the words, meaning the words, to the words themselves.
- Create a vision board, put your affirmations on it, and place it somewhere in your residence where

FOREWORD CONT'D

you will see it multiple times per day. Make a habit of stopping for 30 seconds each time you pass the vision board, pick an affirmation, and read it, either out loud or to yourself.

FemPreneurs, Affirm yourself into more success, into more business, and into a better future! God is preparing You for great things.

Signed,
Dr. Catrina
The Chain Breaker

DR. CATRINA PULLUM

A Louisiana native making a global impact as "The Chain Breaker". An entertainment executive & visionary who is known as "The Whisperer" and "The Negotiator" in the industry. Dr. Catrina's life mission is to help individuals walk in their purpose by creating, igniting, and influencing them to unleash and embrace their power. As a film, television (TV), and theatrical producer, she creates a platform for individuals to share their stories of triumph through the Arts.

Contact her via www.dopegirlfriend.com, www.puissancemaison.com
www.pullcorp.com

FOREWORD

Grace in the Midst of Chaos

It was the beginning of the 5th grade at Park Ridge Elementary and in walks a young girl into an unfamiliar place. She was quiet, humble, and feisty. I had been there since kindergarten though. I knew everyone, all the teachers and every student in the entire building by name yet still shy.

This young girl would give me the courage and tools to navigate the rest of the school year and the many challenges life handed me. "You can't let anyone treat you like that" she would say. I, unassuming and green, would allow everyone to treat me like "that." What is "that" might you ask, well I'll tell you. I was bullied by a brother and sister duo in 3rd, 4th and some of the 5th grade because I didn't have a voice. As our friendship grew, so did my courage to tell the tag team posse to stop.

FOREWORD CONT'D

She inspired me to have hope that the next day, no matter how hard it may be right now, Would always be better when I placed my mind in a positive place. As time progressed and the years passed, I watched her set goals and crush them time after time with that same vigor and positive thinking.

Picture it, Lafayette, LA 1998, she says to me "I'm going to beauty school and run my own salon." Less than 2 years later, it became and still is, a viable, sustainable hair salon business complete with a haircare line. Mother, Author, Serial Entrepreneur, and Visionary are just a few of the many titles she holds. I would say the rest is history but this is her story and it is still being written because there is no stopping Nadia Francois. Her vision of successfully becoming a Mommy Mogul started with

FOREWORD CONT'D

positive thinking and being unafraid to help others along the way.

Research says that when you keep your thoughts positive you can have better mental health, better physical health, success and, happiness. In this book, you will find all of the tools and powerful affirmations to keep you going in the right direction to FemPreneur success.

When I need uplifting, I remember the little girl on the inside of me who overcame being bullied with the help of a wonderful friend who gave life changing advice. That friend reminds me of James, Jesus' brother who was tasked with encouraging, teaching and directing the youth of the church during great persecution. He writes, "Consider it pure joy, my brothers and sisters, whenever you face trials of many kinds, because you

FOREWORD CONT'D

know that the testing of your faith produces perseverance. Let perseverance finish its work so that you may be mature and complete, not lacking anything."

Positive thinking, a wonderful friend, and daily FemPreneur Affirmations will set you on your path to being POWERFUL, ENCOURAGED, and SUCCESSFUL.

Kimberly Rowe,
A Teacher

KIMBERLY ROWE

Kimberly Rowe is an elementary school Teacher at GEO Prep Mid City. She is also a mother of 2 beautiful daughters, and 2 gifted sons. She currently lives in Baker, Louisiana with her wonderful family.

Contact Info:
Email: kim_rowe@outlook.com

PREFACE

This book was developed to empower female "kingdompreneurs" to commit their businesses to Christ, walk by faith and claim victory daily!! The contributing authors want to be an encouragement to other women traveling the journey of entrepreneurship. So they wrote these affirmations and prayers to do just that. There is not a better way to push and motivate others than with God's promises. Powerful Affirmations for FemPreneurs is the success tool for kingdom businesswomen!! We know that the key to success is our faith and prayer life. This book will serve as the pocket-sized pick-me up that all female entrepreneurs can use to get motivated, get focused and get their mindset adjusted for the overflow!!

PRAYER

Dear God in heaven, creator of all things. I come today thanking you for your grace and mercy, thank you for your keeping power. I give you glory, honor and praise today. I thank you for all that you have done and will do in my life. I thank you for my family, friends and enemies. I ask that you bind any forces not sent by you Father, Cover me, my family and my friends in your hedge of protection, Lord. Forgive us for our sins.

Lord, I thank you for my business and I ask that you continue to lead and guide me in all my business decisions and help me to conquer all that you have in store for me. Father, please bless my business associates, team members and collaborations. Lord allow me to be a good steward of your blessings and to always give you the glory. Thank you Lord for your favor and your faithfulness. Help me to be the change I want to see on this earth. In Jesus' name, Amen.

Author Nadia Francois

DAILY AFFIRMATIONS

Suiting Up for Business with the Armor of God

I am strong in the Lord through his power. He has equipped me with everything I need to succeed on my entrepreneurial journey.

God's truth always trumps the lies of the enemy. I will operate my business in integrity and honor, therefore, openly receiving the favor of God.

Through the righteousness of Christ, my prayers are powerful and effective. I will walk in peace and joy knowing that I am covered by grace and mercy.

The peace of God goes before me and paves a wide path to victory. Satan is already defeated, under my feet.

No weapon formed against me shall prosper. For God is my shield and my strength.

DAILY AFFIRMATIONS

Nothing can separate me from the love of Christ. I am more than a conqueror.

I will walk in authority and make my presence known. Confidence is my superpower!!

Author Nadia Francois

"The Lord is my shepherd; I shall not want. He makes me to lie down in [b]green pastures; He leads me beside the [c]still waters. He restores my soul; He leads me in the paths of righteousness For His name's sake. Yea, though I walk through the valley of the shadow of death, I will fear no evil; For You are with me; Your rod and Your staff, they comfort me. You prepare a table before me in the presence of my enemies; You anoint my head with oil; My cup runs over. Surely goodness and mercy shall follow me All the days of my life; And I will dwell in the house of the Lord Forever."

Psalms 23:1-6 NKJV

Nadia Francois

Nadia Lindsey Francois is a serial entrepreneur with a heart for people. A hairstylist by trade, Nadia holds current licenses in Cosmetology and Barbering and a B.S. in Business Administration. The Baton Rouge native began her entrepreneurial journey at the age of 19 and has used her experiences and knowledge to help other business owners start and grow their ventures. Nadia continues to thrive and expand in her beauty endeavors, Heiress Haircare Systems and Heiress Beauty Lounge Online Beauty Supply Boutique which she describes as her passion. Because "people may not always remember what you said but they will always remember how you made them feel." As the founder and Executive

Nadia Francois

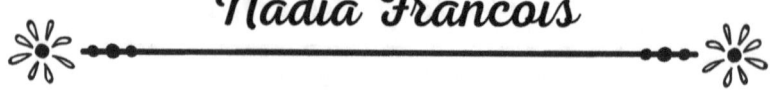

Director of SOE, she has developed a series of programs and workshops that contribute to personal and entrepreneurial growth. Under her leadership, SOE grew from what started as a group of friends who wanted to give countless acts of community service, into a thriving sisterhood that incorporates motivational and business workshops, youth confidence and esteem pageants, and mentorship. The beautypreneur and non-profit founder became a first-time author in August of 2018, publishing The Entrepreneur Activity Workbook as her first project, which is very close to her heart. She created this workbook to help entrepreneurs have a clear business plan and understanding of their business goals. After participating in two additional book projects, Nadia attained the esteemed recognition of International Best Selling Author for Better Woman Better World Book One. Her latest writing project includes her own faith-based compilation, What's Your Super Power Anthology. In December 2020, this trailblazer stepped out on faith and became the channel owner of What's Your

Nadia Francois

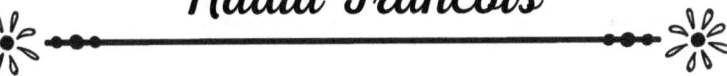

Super Power TV (WYSP TV), which also houses her talk-show by the same title on Exposure TV Network, Nadia and her guest hostesses interview powerhouse women and spotlight minority business owners. The WYSP TV Channel also houses five additional empowering series that span from cooking, spiritual wellness, talk shows and wealth creation. In 2021, Nadia continues to enhance her digital footprint with the addition of Power Conversations Podcast which is another extension of her media empire that caters to entrepreneurs and their advancement. This goal-getter contributes her success to grace and mercy. Her number one assignment is being the mother and sole provider for her four sons, the driving force behind her persistent hustle and diligent pursuit of greatness.

Contact her at
www.nadiafrancois.com
www.sistarsinc.com

PRAYER

Father in Jesus name,

We thank you for Abundance. We pray according to your Word that we can ask and it shall be given, seek, and we shall find and knock and the door shall be opened to us. We thank you that even in the midst of adversaries that profitable, effective, and active doors are opened to us to share your love through our excellence in business.

We thank you that you have:
Broken the chains of lack and want and broken us into a life of the exceeding and abundant. As we step into the new things, we thank you that you have locked the doors of poverty and lack in all areas of our lives including spiritual, natural, financial, health, mental, social and relationships behind us as we

 # PRAYER CONT'D

continue to tap into the treasure of your Word. We thank you and pray that multiple streams of abundance are uncovered and tapped as we grow in our relationship with you.

We thank you that after we have labored in our businesses and ministries that our baskets are full and our store has plenty to share. We thank you for giving us seed to sow into your kingdom and to those in need.

We recognize that you have unlocked the power to get wealth unto us through divine connections, divine downloads, and divine strategies. We thank you for the staff and the help sent to sustain this growth.

PRAYER CONT'D

You have placed our name in the wind and it is landing on the desks and lips of decision-makers, destiny partners, bankers, funders, angel investors, and agents. We thank you that their pens are filled with ink and they are ready to sign contracts, sales orders, and checks.

We are so thankful that we can't help but praise you In advance for the blessings. We are assured that you do not lie and the good work you have begun in us will be fully performed to your glory.

In Jesus' Name
Amen

Author Celeste Payne

DAILY AFFIRMATIONS

Affirming Awareness, Attraction and Abundance

I AM ABUNDANCE therefore I emanate love, generosity and more than enough wherever I go.

I live thankful. My life is one beautiful adventurous flow of joy, goodness and harmony and I bring that flow and gratitude to my business and all my endeavors.

I attract clients that can render payment for the services I provide with no delay. Success is sure for me and my business. I circulate money with ease and am elated to pay those who render services to me.

My awareness and discernment are keen. I have the insight, wisdom and knowledge to make the best decisions for my life and business.

I attract money every day. It comes to me in increasing quantities, quickly, easily and, continuously from multiple sources. I get to keep, circulate, and give it with pleasure.

DAILY AFFIRMATIONS

My clients are satisfied and successful so therefore they always refer me to others for more business, projects and blessed opportunities.

I am creative, it is my God given ability. I sow into purposeful people and projects including myself and I continue to grow by being a lifelong learner.

Author Tonia Askins

"And He said to me, "My grace is sufficient for you, for My strength is made perfect in weakness." Therefore most gladly I will rather boast in my infirmities, that the power of Christ may rest upon me."

2 Corinthians 2:9 NKJV

Tonia Askins

The Freedom Teacher, Tonia Askins is an international business consultant, book publisher, TV show producer and Louisiana State Director for SCORE. She has served emerging entrepreneurs, nonprofits, existing small business owners and corporations for over twenty years globally. "I fuel people to do three things: be creative, sow and grow. Be Creative about how you go about achieving your goals, sow into purposeful projects that help others and grow by continually remaining a student of life." When she is not creating strategic plans for organizations, preparing

Tonia Askins

for her next speaking engagement or working with authors, developing new books, she is at home enjoying her 3 kids and husband of over 20 years, likely scoping out where the next live Jazz or R&B band will be performing for some relaxation.

Contact her at
1-866-5LetsGo (53-8746)
www.thefreedomteacher.com
IG @MoneyEverydayTV
IG @TheFreedomTeacher

 # PRAYER

Father God, I pray your blessings upon every female entrepreneur. Fill each of us with wisdom, knowledge and full understanding. Grant us your favor and place us before people of great influence in order to take our businesses to the next level. Thank you for divine connections. Lord, enlarge our territory. Allow each of us to be fully successful. Lord, you are great and you are greatly to be praised. Lord God, thank you for making us unstoppable women! In Jesus Name, Amen

Author Dana Ayo

DAILY AFFIRMATIONS

Dana's Femfirmations

I Am Royalty.

I Am Successful.

I Am Maintained By God.

I Am Unstoppable.

I Am Worth It.

I Am A Money Magnet.

I Don't Make Excuses, I Make It Happen.

Author Dana Ayo

"I Can Do All Things Through Christ Who Strengthens Me."

　　　　　　　Phillipians 4:13 NKJV

Dana Ayo

Dana A. Ayo is a single mother with one adult daughter who has been her motivation in life. Dana's unwavering determination to provide a stable living environment for her daughter and to break the stigma of single parent households has been her driving force. Dana is a natural born encourager and she is passionate about the people and things that she holds close to her heart. Dana absolutely adores her family and is a lover of God! Dana is an independent businesswoman. She is an accomplished rhinestone designer with an eye for fashion.

Dana Ayo

She is the CEO of HD Bling t-shirts and accessories which specializes in creating beautifully rhinestone embellished clothing and accessories. Dana's commitment is to help women proclaim who they are and to proclaim where they are going. She is also committed to assisting business owners in further marketing their brands through the artistry of BLING.

Contact her at
www.hdbling.com
www.hdroyaltees.com
@hdbling @hdroyaltees

PRAYER

Heavenly Father, I come before you with a heart filled with thanksgiving. Your love is everlasting. Lord I thank you for your word which is a lamp to my feet and a lamp to my path. Lord I thank you for the host of warring and ministering angels that war on behalf of me and everyone connected to me. Lord I thank you for peace, that passes all understanding. Lord I thank you, for the Grace that is on my life to accomplish all that you have for to me to do. All glory and honor to you in all that I do. Amen

Author Feleshia Borskey-Young

DAILY AFFIRMATIONS

Crowned with Purpose

I define my worth and I am worthy of all God has for me!

I am not broken, God made stained glass out of my brokenness.

Wake Up, Pray Up, Level Up—-Reposition for Purpose.

I'm coming for everything they said I couldn't have.

Problems feed on fear. Blessings feed on faith. I am fueled by faith.

I will Balance tasks by taking on what I can handle, not the hassle.

The crown was fit for me. I wear it with Pride and keep God on my side.

Author Breonna Baker

"Behold, I give you the authority to trample on serpents and scorpions, and over all the power of the enemy, and nothing shall by any means hurt you."   Luke 10:19

Breonna Baker

Breonna Baker is wife, educator and business consultant. Breonna and her husband have a podcast together, Resilient Love Podcast where they discuss love, life and business. She is the owner of Streamline Media Agency, LLC which is a social media management and business consulting company. Breonna just loves family and desires to fulfill her God-given purpose.

Contact her at
@mrsbreonnabaker
@resilientlovepodcast

PRAYER

Father God, in the Name of Jesus, I thank you for the grace upon the life of every entrepreneur. Give them creative ideas, thoughts, and imaginations to carry out the visions you have placed upon their hearts. Activate their gifts in great measure, causing them to be successful in their craft. Also, open their spiritual eyes to see your hand at work, as they move forward. Set a fire in their hearts, to motivate and encourage them as they establish your plan and purpose. And thank you for the resources needed to make their visions a reality and to bring you Glory!

In Jesus' Name, Amen!

Author Tonya Hilliard Battieste

DAILY AFFIRMATIONS

I Frame My World with My Words!

I live in my present and leave my past behind.

I acknowledge my own self-worth.

I am capable, confident, and committed.

I am in the process of becoming the best version of myself.

The word of God is my direction and the presence of God is my peace.

My strength is greater than my struggle.

My thoughts are filled with positivity and my life is plentiful with prosperity.

Author Tonya Hilliard Battieste

"Seek the Kingdom of God above all else, and live righteously, and he will give you everything you need."

Matthew 6:33 NLT

Dr. Tonya Hilliard Battieste

Dr. Tonya Renne Hilliard Battieste is an intercessor, motivator, Kingdom philanthropist and ministry leader. As a Louisiana native, born and raised in Baton Rouge, Dr. Hillard Battieste has a great love for Southern cuisine and culture. In 2020, she earned a doctoral degree in Biblical Psychology from Hope Bible Institute, Baton Rouge Campus, and currently serves as a Pastor at Heavenly H.OP.E. Ministries in Baton Rouge. As a mother, mother-in-love, and grandmother, Dr. Hilliard

Dr. Tonya Hilliard Battieste

Battieste enjoys spending time with family and loved ones. A trailblazer with a calling to advance the Kingdom of God, her vision is to create an outpost of heaven on earth.

Contact her at tbattieste@gmail.com

PRAYER

Lord God, may we always have the liberty to walk in peace that surpasses all understanding, knowing that you are always going before us fighting our battles and causing us to win. In Jesus name, Amen.

Author Vashiti Bratton

DAILY AFFIRMATIONS

Living Victoriously

Walk in Peace and let the Lord fight your Battles.

Stay True to God and He will always be True to you.

Changing my thoughts will Change my life.

Giving is living, our level of Giving will determine our level of living.

Don't get right, Stay right.

When God restores what has been broken in my life, the end result is Amazing, better than new.

I am Blessed to be a Blessing.

Author Vashiti Bratton

"Trust in the Lord with all your heart,
And lean not on your own understanding;
6 In all your ways acknowledge Him,
And He shall direct your paths."
                    Proverbs 3:5-6 NKJV

Vashiti Bratton

Elder Vashiti Bratton is an honorable woman of God and a dynamic preacher/teacher of the precious word of God, as well as a mentor to many. She is adamant about empowering God's people to live a victorious life of Holiness by rightly dividing the word of God, in such a way that it will impact God's people while bringing health, healing, and deliverance to the listeners. Elder Bratton leads by example as she walks in love with all that she comes in contact with. She believes that the word of God is truth and it has the

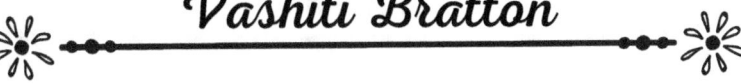

ability to set us free from any form of bondage while causing us to live holy and acceptable unto God, without compromising the word of God.

Contact her at
vashitibratton@msn.com
www.coveredgirls.net

PRAYER

Heavenly Father, I thank you for every female entrepreneur and I cover them in prayer. You have given them the desire to be their own boss, along with the grace and imagination that they will need to bring their visions and dreams to pass. Open new doors for them and increase their presence in the entrepreneurial arena. Guide every business decision leading them to great success and prosperity. Please help them to be bold and courageous as they work to bring wealth and riches into manifestation in their own lives and empower them to be a voice of encouragement and support to other women who have chosen this path as well. I ask these blessings from you, for my sisters. In Jesus name, Amen.

Author Tonya Hilliard Battieste

DAILY AFFIRMATIONS

Affirmations for a Spiritual Mentality

I am a child of the Most High God.

I am beautiful inside and out.

I am a woman of purpose. God has a plan and a hope for me and I will walk daily in that purpose.

I am dressed for success. I am clothed in strength and dignity.

I am protected. The Holy Spirit surrounds me from head to toe.

God has my back. If God be for me who shall be against me.

I have a faith that does not quit.

Author Angelica Carmouche

"Therefore I say to you, whatever things you ask when you pray, believe that you receive them, and you will have them."

Mark 11:24 NKJV

Angelica Carmouche

Founder of Kiss My Soap and Angel Market, Angelica Carmouche is US Navy Veteran, a soap maker and author of short children stories. She is currently working on her first novel Soul Flames. Mom to two boys, she finds solace in God, family and the family dog King.

Contact her at
angeldrisana@gmail.com

PRAYER

Father God, In the name of Jesus. I humbly come before your throne of Grace. Thanking you for your son Jesus, who died that we would have life more abundantly. Father, I yet praise your name for what you are doing in my business. Lord, I thank you for the growth, the abundance, provision, the customers and the clients. Lord, I decree and declare that I have everything I need, according to your riches in glory through Christ Jesus. Lord, I receive the overflow. God, I thank you for the wisdom and discernment in Jesus name. Amen.

Author Elizabeth Crawford

DAILY AFFIRMATIONS

God's QUEENDOM Woman

I am passionate about positioning myself to pursue purpose.

I am NOT distracted by Destiny Derailers or Dream Bandits.

You possess what the World requests.

You were crowned a Conqueror and a Champion.

I operate in God Inspired Direction and Creative Power.

I attract Divine Connections to my Life.

As long as I have Breath in My Body, God has a Plan and a Purpose for me.

Author Elizabeth Crawford

"Beloved, I pray that you may prosper in all things and be in health, just as your soul prospers."

3 John 2 NKJV

Elizabeth Crawford

Elizabeth Crawford or Coach Liz is a Certified Career and Personal Development Coach, Global Career Development Facilitator, National and International Best Selling Author, Speaker, Consultant and Entrepreneur. She is the CEO of Wisdom & Insights LLC. Coach Liz helps women who are battling; stress, fatigue, burn-out, Imposter Syndrome, Analysis Paralysis and Limiting Beliefs.

Contact her at
www.wisdomforlife101.com @selfinvest101
Email:wisdomforlife101@gmail.com

PRAYER

Most High God I thank you for who you are the author and finisher of my faith. My Alpha and Omega my beginning and the end. Only through you can I embrace your perfect will on earth as it is in heaven. Here I am your servant ready to obey. For your word says obedience is better than sacrifice. I lift my eyes to the hills whence my help come from the Lord. I shall fear no evil for thou art with me. Thou has prepared a table before me in the presence of my enemies. You anoint my head with oil my cup runs over. Goodness and mercy shall follow me all the days of my life. I wait patiently for the Lord, He will renew my strength. I shall be like the tree planted by living waters that shall bear fruit in due season I shall prosper. I will dwell in the house of the Lord. In Jesus name Amen.

Author Enola Pillard

DAILY AFFIRMATIONS

I am who He said, not what they said

My past isn't an indicator of my future.

I am an asset and not a liability.

I am more than enough.

I am the hands and feet of Jesus.

I am someone's answered prayer.

I am an overcomer.

I am investment worthy.

Author Monica Jones

"For I, the Lord your God, will hold your right hand, Saying to you, 'Fear not, I will help you."

Isaiah 41:13

Monica Jones

Monica Regina Jones. is an ordained minister and serves at Sons of Isaachar Ministries in her hometown of Kinston North Carolina. She is a frontline worker in the department of Environmental Services at UNC Lenoir Hospital. She is an author of four books: God's Humble Voice, Transparency Heals, Surrendered Vessels, and a co-author with Carla R. Cannon, in the book Turbulence.

Contact her at jonesmonica564@yahoo.com

PRAYER

Lord God, I'm not looking to the left nor to the right, my eyes are fixed on Jesus and I know and appreciate that You have my best interest at heart and will always be wherever I need you, omnipotent father. In Jesus name, Amen.

Author Vashiti Bratton

DAILY AFFIRMATIONS

"Sis"

Sis, you were given a vision for your life not as an option, but as a directive. It is your reason for being. It's time to stop playing small and start living your purpose.

Sis, not everyone will understand your vision. It is not theirs to get. It's YOURS. Stop seeking validation from the world. Tune in to the spirit within YOU and pursue your calling diligently.

Sis, remember that every dream you've been given comes with a path to manifestation. You were born for this and blessed with the power to achieve it.

Sis, sometimes blessings come dressed as tragedies. Instead of being anxious, be grateful. You are being called to greatness.

DAILY AFFIRMATIONS

Sis, do not let fear keep you stagnant. You may be unsure of what your next step should be or where it will lead. Take it anyway.

Sis, your comfort zone is your enemy. Stop sitting on your gifts. Start believing in yourself and take action.

Sis, the time to shine is now. Your season is here. Stop "waiting for a sign". The world is waiting on YOU.

Author Marilyn Oduenyi

"Fear not, for I am with you; Be not dismayed, for I am your God. I will strengthen you, Yes, I will help you,
I will uphold you with My righteous right hand."

Isaiah 41:10 NKJV

Marilyn Oduenyi

Marilyn is a Wife, Mother of three, Cognitive Behavioral Therapist, Speaker, Author, Transformational Motherhood Coach & Life Strategist. She is the founder of The Peaceful Black Mama where she helps Black mothers change the narrative and rise above social stereotypes about who they are to find true freedom through mastering their mindset, healing their relationships and taking control of their financial future. Her mission is to empower moms to find their peace, discover their purpose and claim their power to not only

Marilyn Oduenyi

survive motherhood but to transform it into the platform from which they shine. Marilyn's work with Black mothers has been featured on NBC, CBS & Fox News.

Contact her at
www.thepeacefulblackmama.com

PRAYER

Father, I thank you for sharing a portion of your creative power. n you, all of my creativity originates (Gen.1:1). Today, I tap into the river of your creativity to solve problems. My creativity is on assignment. Therefore, I thank you that my gifts and talents meet a need, fulfil a vision and bring a living hope to someone's life. Today I call on all of the benefits of Psalm 103. I thank you that I am healthy, free from disease and is conditioned to carry out our assignment today. I thank you that my mind is clear and focused (Is 26:3). I thank you that my heart is sensitive to the promptings of the Holy Spirit. I lay aside every weight and obstacle (Hebrews 12:). I pull down every stronghold that is assigned to deter my focus and steal my creative energy (2 Corinthians 10:4). I thank you that doors are open for me to join you in the work you are already doing

PRAYER CONT'D

on earth. Father, help me to work efficiently and effectively showing my faith and my trust in you by my works (James 2:18). Allow my efforts to be organized and line up in the order that achieves optimal results. I thank you that when our assignment is complete, that according to Matthew 14:20 I experience "chortazo," the fullness that comes after I serve. Allow my basket to be full and let overflow remain in my home and business so that I have enough to maintain, sustain, sow, and share. Allow me to enjoy the fruits of our labor together with the Lord evidenced by a life that is abundant and full. Let me be ever mindful of your creative provision and let me always give you glory for what is created as a result of our partnership. For all of this Lord I give you praise, honor and glory, In Jesus Name. Amen

Author Celeste Payne

DAILY AFFIRMATIONS

Affirmations of Creativity

My body and health are fit for this Kingdom Marketplace assignment. My diet, immune system, and all of my biological systems are in line to support this creative work and don't hinder my progress.

I hear clearly from God regarding business opportunities, and creative decisions. I am prepared and sensitive to the promptings of the Holy Spirit and move as He guides.

My creativity solves problems for my customers. I tap into divine strategies and systems. I tap into creative rivers and discover witty inventions.

My creativity causes an increase in my life. I have consistent and reliable income and do not stress about money. Daily hundreds of dollars are deposited from clients, customers, sponsors and more. I ask God for what I need and He creates the supply.

DAILY AFFIRMATIONS

Today, creative ideas are flowing for me. These ideas are unique, innovative, effective and divine gateways and divine connections.

My creativity creates times to enjoy life. Since I work hard, I play hard and enjoy the fruits of my labor.

I am well balanced and organized. My day is planned and I accomplish all of my daily goals. This organization enables my creative ideas to flourish.

Author Celeste Payne

"For I know the thoughts that I think toward you, says the Lord, thoughts of peace and not of evil, to give you a future and a hope."

Jeremiah 29:11 NKJV

Celeste Payne

Celeste M. Payne is an artist, author, educator, entrepreneur. She is the founder The WOW Pages for Business & Professional Women, an interactive directory. This online community is designed to allow its members to network with like-minded professionals, share their products & services, shop with other women in business, and grow personally and professionally through. She is the author of "I Love Me Some Me" and a library other ebooks, and creator of art,

Celeste Payne

and apparel. Though life has not been easy. Through her relationship with God, Celeste has developed the fortitude to overcome by becoming the encouraging voice that she missed. She transfers that passion into her work and speaking engagements by giving hope and courage to the women she encounters.

Contact her at
www.celesteempowers.com
www.theWOWpages.com

 # PRAYER

Thank you for renewing my mind through your word and lining my thoughts up with your word and letting me know that I know, it's a new day, it's a new way, and it's a new will for my life, in Jesus name, Amen

Author Vashiti Bratton

DAILY AFFIRMATIONS

Mrs. Peppers Quotes

Preparation is preparation no matter how you prepare.

Trying something new doesn't mean that's who you are.

I'm slowly becoming the person I should've been long time ago.

Knowing who you are is the biggest reward you can give yourself.

Knowing the end always make the beginning understandable.

Redundancy makes permanency.

Over prepared is like, over cooked rice.

Author Ernee Peppers

"Then the Lord answered me and said: "Write the vision And make it plain on tablets, That he may run who reads it."
Habakkuk 2:2 NKJV

Ernee Peppers

Born in Harlem but raised in Trinidad and Brooklyn, NY and can remember falling head over heels for speaking in front of an audience. Ernee's contagious energy was an impressive example of what a true stage presence should be guaranteed to an audience which she believes should be filled with a whirlwind full of laughs and memorable characters. Ernee Peppers – Award Winning Talk Show Host, Best Selling Author, Relationship Coach & Strategist, Publisher, Public Speaker, and Entrepreneur has distinguished herself in

Ernee Peppers

much more authentic roles, namely as a wife, mom– and a highly-acclaimed business woman which has truly lifts her profile way above the stars. Ernee has always embraced her eclecicity, fabulosity, creativity, extraordinaire and amplified "YASSSS BABY!" with a style and class that has shown absolutely no signs of slowing down.

Contact her at
theerneepeppersshow@gmail.com

PRAYER

Father, I lift my hands to thee. Thanks for the gift you have placed in my hand. In your word you promise to open the windows of heaven and pour out your blessings. Make me the head, not the tail; above only, not beneath; a lender, not a borrower. I will forever lift holy hands to honor you for all you have done and plan to do. Believing my faith will move mountains, I declare and decree that everything that belongs to me by divine right will be released. I will pray without ceasing knowing the prayers of the righteous availeth much. Order my steps according to your purpose and plan for my life. I totally submit to your will and your way. In Jesus name, Amen.

Author Enola Pillard

DAILY AFFIRMATIONS

My Cup Runneth Over

I walk with power and authority whatever I speak shall come to pass.

Each creative idea will draw me closer to my destiny.

Greatness surround me like a shield.

Everyone of my dreams will become my reality.

Miracles coming my way suddenly, speedily, immediately, quickly and in the same hour.

Effort and determination will lead me to my promise land.

I excel in all I do my steps ordered by the Lord. My mind is free and open to new possibilities.

Author Enola Pillard

Rejoice always, pray without ceasing, in everything give thanks; for this is the will of God in Christ Jesus for you.

I Thessalonians 5:16-18

Dr. Enola Pillard

Dr. Enola Pillard, D.P.C. is the CEO/Founder of Ashanti Enterprises. She is a professional hair stylist, business owner, educator, life coach. inspirational consultant and author of the book, Adjusting Your Crown. It is a book written to encourage and inspire individuals to establish their vision, set their goals, make adjustments daily if necessary; then accomplish those goals and fulfill their vision through hard work and trust in God.

Contact her at www.ashantienterprises.com

 # PRAYER

Our Father and Our God, as you shower me with your blessings and favor, grant me the grace to love like you love and the ability to give like you give from the heart. May I always be in the position to answer a need in someone else's life and be a blessing to many. In Jesus name, Amen.

Author Vashiti Bratton

DAILY AFFIRMATIONS

Be Responsible for Who You Truly Are

The road to reinvention starts with you forgiving yourself for your transgressions and giving you license to be human and make mistakes.

Never treat anyone better than they treat you, it dishonors you and the respect that you have for yourself. You are not required to think more of anyone than they think of you.

When you are tired of hurting, make a strong commitment towards happiness and let nothing deter you from that journey.

You have a responsibility to love yourself wholeheartedly, to aspire to be great, even when you don't feel great; to climb the highest mountain, even when your legs hurt, there will always be a reason not to do something, or someone or something telling you, you can't do something.

DAILY AFFIRMATIONS

But determination can be the motivator that changes your mood and puts a boost in your legs. Be Your Own Driving Force.

Anyone that is not supporting you on your journey, is in fact that obstacle that is in the way of your journey.

The road to success is paved with many ups and downs and many mistakes and bad decisions, each mishap will bring you closer to the finish line, so make mistakes, it means you are taking healthy risks and trying new things.

Set Boundaries for yourself and everyone in your life, it creates order and garners respect.

Author Tamuri Richardson

"who show the work of the law written in their hearts, their conscience also bearing witness, and between themselves their thoughts accusing or else excusing them"

Romans 2:15 NKJV

Tamuri Richardson

Tamuri Richardson is an International Best Selling Author, Professional Motivational Speaker, Communications Specialist, Certified Mental Health Advocate, Influential Storyteller, and Domestic Violence Conqueror.

Contact at www.tleannespeaks.com

 # PRAYER

Father God in the name of Jesus I thank you Lord. Thank you for being the Lord and head of my life. Thank you for being an ever present help in my time of need. Lord you are great and greatly to be praise. God I thank you for the assignment that is on my life. I thank you for giving me purpose and vision. And I thank you for the provision to get it done. It is you God that gives the power to get wealth. In Jesus name. Amen

Author Feleshia B. Young

DAILY AFFIRMATIONS

God's Path to Success In Him

I am truly enough to complete the assignment God gave me in life.

I am on the right path at the right time.

I will commit to serving others.

I am a blessing To others.

Stay on the path because it is the light that is leading me to my destiny.

God started a good work in me and He will carry it through to completion.

I am strong because Jesus made me strong.

Author Sandra Sanders

"Being confident of this very thing, that He who has begun a good work in you will complete it until the day of Jesus Christ;"

Phillipians 1:6 NKJV

Sandra Sanders

Sandy Sanders is a 3x International Best-selling author, motivational speaker, advocate, and CEO and founder of social media talk syndication, Coffee Conversations with Sandy and Friends and Book Talks with Sandy, a culture-savvy segment and conversationalists. She addressing, covering, and challenging souls, who need it most; through the power of conversation. Sandy speaks of overcoming a traumatic childhood, low self-esteem, alcoholism and domestic violence, has given Sandy a great sense of relation with communal advocacy.

Contact her at booktalkswithsandy@gmail.com
www.coffeeconversationswithsandy.com

PRAYER

Dear Lord, my prayer today is for every woman who has taken on the mantle to start her own business. I ask you now to be the voice in their ear, reminding them that they can do all things in your strength. Inspiration and creativity is their portion, and all of heaven's resources are available to them because you are their provider. With passion and grace, their visions will be birthed into the earth and will be a blessing to all who partake of them. Favor shall go before them as they blaze the trail of success for their present and future. FemPreneurs, you got this, the Lord is with you and for you! Go forth and do great things! In Jesus name, Amen.

Author Tonya Hilliard Battieste

DAILY AFFIRMATIONS
Sunshine's Words of Wisdom

Always be a first-rate version of yourself not a second-rate version of someone else.

I am a melanin queen with the heart of a lioness.

How you can compete when you don't compare?

My biggest competition is me.

Strive to be a blessing to someone new each and every day.

God first, family second, career third.

Know your worth then add tax!

Author Adrian Smith

"Be anxious for nothing, but in everything by prayer and supplication, with thanksgiving, let your requests be made known to God; and the peace of God, which surpasses all understanding, will guard your hearts and minds through Christ Jesus."

Philippians 4:6-9 NKJV

Adrian Smith

Adrian Smith is a mother of 3 and Mary Kay senior beauty consultant for 5 years. She owns a travel business, is a project manager for an insurance company and also sells health and wellness products including CBD cream, teas and more.

Contact her at
Www.marykay.com/asmith81881
adriansmith81.inteletravel.com

PRAYER

Father we thank you that you always hear us. Today we ask that every affirmation for love, identity, and business is heard, sealed, and blessed by you. God we decree that no enemy near or far has power over the ordained path you've chosen for me. God you said in your word that I am the head and not the tail, the lender and not the borrow, above and not beneath and today I decree your word will arise in my life. Your word breaks and destroys every generational curse and every word negative generational habit. I decree that I am the game changer in my family for generations to come. I decreed that I am blessed beyond measure. Thank you for divine manifestation. In Jesus name, Amen.

Author Dionne Smith

DAILY AFFIRMATIONS

I Am Whole

I am worthy of love, kindness, and compassion and it comes to me easily.

I am fully present in every moment that brings me blessings and goodness.

I achieve all of my goals and nothing will hinder me.

My positivity changes atmospheres, breaks generational curses, and calls blessings to flow to me.

I am walking into the greatest season of my life without fear, reservation, and negative self talk.

I am completely forgiven by God and Myself for past mistakes as I walk in the freedom of God's unconditional love.

All shackles of shame, failure, and defeat are broken off of my life.

Author Dionne Smith

Dr. Dionne Smith

Dr. Dionne Smith is a Co-Pastor, Licensed Professional Counselor, and National Certified Counselor who has a sincere passion for being an agent of change to individuals who are suffering emotionally, mentally, and spiritually. In 2017, she launched two businesses, Made Whole Counseling, LLC and "MotivateMeDee" which focuses on empowering women, motivational mentorship and providing therapeutic treatment. In 2018 she became a LPC-S (Licensed Professional Counselor-Supervisor) to provide supervision, support, and education to counselor interns.

Dr. Dionne Smith

In May 2021, Dionne received her Doctorate of Biblical Psychology. Dionne will forever be committed to serving the community with mental & spiritual health services through therapy, training, and education. Dionne is married to Bishop Michael Smith Sr and loving mother of two children (Victoria 23yrs old & Michael 7yrs old). She stands on the scripture, " Psalm 27:13-14, I had fainted, unless I had believed to see the goodness of the Lord in the land of the living. Wait on the Lord: be of good courage, and he shall strengthen thine heart: wait, I say, on the Lord."

Contact her at
www.madewholecounseling.com

PRAYER

Almighty God, my way maker I pray that you order my steps and position my feet to prosper. I lean and depend upon you, trusting you with all my heart, mind and soul. Father receive my praise and worship as I pour my love on thee. I'm holding on to your word and promises. As I sit in the seat of expectancy, I believe you will show up strong and mighty. You have never let me down. Jehovah Jireh my great provider I know you heard my cry as I made my petition known. I thank you in advance. In Jesus name. Amen.

Author Enola Pillard

DAILY AFFIRMATIONS

I Manifest!

Today will be a Great Day!

I am making today count.

I will not worry about things I cannot control.

I am like no one else.

I never give up.

I will stay positive!

I am happy!

Author Thinitra Smith

"With a strong hand, and with an outstretched arm,
For His mercy endures forever;"
                                    Psalms 136:12

Thinitra Smith

Thinitra Smith is a Louisiana native, and a seasoned real estate professional of 17 years. She recognizes and value the trust her clients place in her and strive every day to exceed their expectations. Thinitra always had a passion to help others and found her true calling in real estate serving her clients and guiding them through one of the biggest investments of their lives. Outside of real estate, she takes pride in giving back to the community and serves as a Board Member of Sistars Of Empowerment non- profit organization.

Contact her at www.thinitrasmith.com

PRAYER

Pray this prayer with me:

Heavenly Father, I come to you in the name of Jesus I reverence you as my Lord and my Savior. You are the great I am, any and everything I need I can find it in you. Thank you for your amazing grace and your unfailing love. I thank you for your will and plans for my life. Help me to be all that you called and predestined me to be. I believe in your word concerning my life, I trust you to do exceedingly, abundantly above all that I can ask or think according to the power that works in me. Help me to stay humbled under your mighty hand and help me to keep my faith active as your promises unfold in my life in Jesus powerful name, Amen.

Author Shanika Stewart

DAILY AFFIRMATIONS

Sis Now it's Your Turn To Thrive

Sis you are anointed and amazing.

Sis you are a wealth magnet.

Sis you survived now thrive.

Sis you are the one God chosen.

Sis you are favored by God.

Sis you are protected by God.

Sis you are full of the wisdom of God.

Author Shanika Stewart

"Now to Him who is able to do exceedingly abundantly above all that we ask or think, according to the power that works in us,"
     Ephesians 3:20 NKJV

Dr. Shanika Stewart

Co-Pastor Prophetess Shanika Stewart is a resident of Zachary La and is married to Pastor Anthony Stewart of Active Faith Christian Center of Baton Rouge La. Stewart has 2 beautiful children and 4 amazing grandchildren. Stewart dedicates her life to the call that God has purposed and will for her life. Stewart has been serving effectively for 10yrs and don't plan on stopping until Jesus return. Besides being a wife, mother , daughter and friend Stewart is also a business owner, author of 2 books "The Wounded Shall Recover, The Benefits of your Release" and is currently

Dr. Shanika Stewart

working on a collaboration project allowing people to share their stories or share wisdom nuggets on how to come out of poverty into the Promises of God. Stewart is a worshipper, intercessor , prayer warrior and a minister of the gospel. Stewart has her Doctorate in Biblical Psychology where she enjoy Christian Counseling. Where she believes counseling is a great launching path to THRIVE. Stewart is the visionary of Women of Faith and Hope Ministry.

Stewart's mission is to help change lives through the spoken word of God and also by being the hands and feet willing to get the job done representing-the Kingdom of Heaven as one of God's Ambassadors . Her favorite question to ask is "is your faith active?" If so together we will Thrive

Contact her at
www.1anointedtouchapparel.com

PRAYER

Our Father and Our God, as you shower me with your blessings and favor, grant me the grace to love, like you love and the ability to give, like you give from the heart. May I always be in the position to answer a need in someone else's life and be a blessing to many. In Jesus name, Amen.

Author Vashiti Bratton

DAILY AFFIRMATIONS

I Am!!

I Am brave.

I Am part of the breath of life.

I Am fearless.

I Am enough.

I Am from the great I AM ,

I Am resourceful.

I dream, I believe, I receive.

Author Tosha White

"And the Scripture was fulfilled which says, "Abraham believed God, and it was accounted to him for righteousness." And he was called the friend of God."

James 2:23 NKJV

Tosha White

Tosha White, raised in Carencro, Louisiana is the mother of two biological children, and three honorary: Monica, Lonnie, and Benjamin. She is also Founder of Non Profit "Let's Talk about it.". Tosha works as a Medical Office Assistant, is an Author and Spiritual Life Coach.

Contact her at
www.toshawhite.com

PRAYER

Father God in the name of Jesus, I give you glory for every divinely inspired idea and witty invention. Father I thank you for the grace to accomplish all that I set out to do according to your will. I declare now that my business is blessed that my sister's business is blessed. Father I thank you that it is you that has given me the power to get wealth. I thank you that no weapon formed against me or my business can prosper. Lord, I thank you for your angels that go before me to make crooked places straight. Thank you for opening all the spiritual and natural doors that I need opened and closing the doors that are not meant to prosper me. Lord I thank you that I can do all things with you. God, Remind me that I am unstoppable when I start to let weariness and fear in. I thank you that you walk with

PRAYER CONT'D

me every step aligning me with the people and places that will propel me to the destiny you have for me. Father thank you that all things work for my good and I fear nothing. I give you all the honor and the praise for all you have done and all you are doing. In Jesus name. Amen

Author Feleshia B. Young

"For though we walk in the flesh, we do not war according to the flesh. **4** For the weapons of our warfare are not [a]carnal but mighty in God for pulling down strongholds, **5** casting down arguments and every high thing that exalts itself against the knowledge of God, bringing every thought into captivity to the obedience of Christ"

2 Corinthians 10:3-5 NKJV

DAILY AFFIRMATIONS

Passion and Purpose for the Promises of God

Everyday I strive for progress and perfection will come.

I believe I can so I will.

I crucify the part of me that embraces fear so that courage and boldness continues to manifest.

I fight for what I want now so I don't have to fight against what I don't want later.

I ride the waves because smooth waters never produce skilled sailors.

I put on the full amour of God and I am fully protected from the enemies evil strategies.

My heart is pure and free from UNforgiveness for my enemy is not flesh and blood, but it is the evil powers and rulers of this world and designed to keep me from fulfilling my God given purpose.

Author Feleshia B. Young

Dr. Feleshia Borskey Young

Prophetess Feleshia Borskey-Young is the First Lady of Heavenly Hope Ministries, a Licensed Professional Christian Therapist, a Minister, a Motivational Speaker, an Author, and a visionary. She is the Founder of the 411ForWomen Outreach Organization and the 411ForWomen Foundation. This organization is dedicated to women and children who have been victims of domestic and intimate partner violence. Dr. B Young has accepted her life's assignment to inspire, motivate, and edify others. As a survivor of Domestic Violence and teenage pregnancy,

Dr. Feleshia Borskey Young

Dr. B Young is passionate about serving the people of God, especially His daughters. Dr. Young understands the courage and support required to overcome such unfortunate and evil circumstances. Dr. Young avails herself to every opportunity to present the truth and dispel the lies that encourage self-hate, neglected potential, abuse, and unhealthy kingdom marriages. Above all her accomplishments Dr. Young considers supporting her husband Bishop Johnny B Young, in ministry and guiding her children Cordarryl, Kelsei Jairean and Rushaad to be valuable assets to the Kingdom of God and Society alike, as her primary purpose.

Contact her at
www.feleshiaborskeyyoung.com
www.411forwomen.com
www.firstladyconcepts.com

www.ingramcontent.com/pod-product-compliance
Lightning Source LLC
Chambersburg PA
CBHW050243220526
45465CB00002B/526